yoko tsuno
electronics engineer

by Roger Leloup

THE PREY AND THE GHOST

9th CINEBOOK
The 9th Art Publisher

Original title: Yoko Tsuno 12 – La Proie et l'ombre

Original edition: © Dupuis, 1982 by Roger Leloup
www.dupuis.com

English translation: © 2008 Cinebook Ltd

Translator: Jerome Saincantin
Lettering and text layout: Imadjinn sarl
Printed in Spain by Just Colour Graphic

This edition first published in Great Britain in 2008 by
Cinebook Ltd
56 Beech Avenue
Canterbury, Kent
CT4 7TA
www.cinebook.com

A CIP catalogue record for this book
is available from the British Library

ISBN 978-1-905460-56-4

ON AN AUTUMN EVENING, ON A SCOTTISH ROAD.

HEY! EASY THERE! AND KEEP LEFT. WE'RE IN SCOTLAND!

I DON'T SEE HOW I COULD KEEP LEFT ON A ROAD...

... WHERE THERE IS ONLY ROOM FOR ONE CAR! YOU GOT THE DIRECTIONS WRONG.

WRONG, ME? WE'RE ABOUT TO REACH A CASTLE AND... OH? THERE ARE TWO CASTLES. THIS MAP IS STUPID.

YOU'LL HAVE TO HEAD BACK AND TAKE THE FIRST LEFT.

HEAD BACK? AS SOON AS I CAN... HEY! WHAT...?

WHOA!

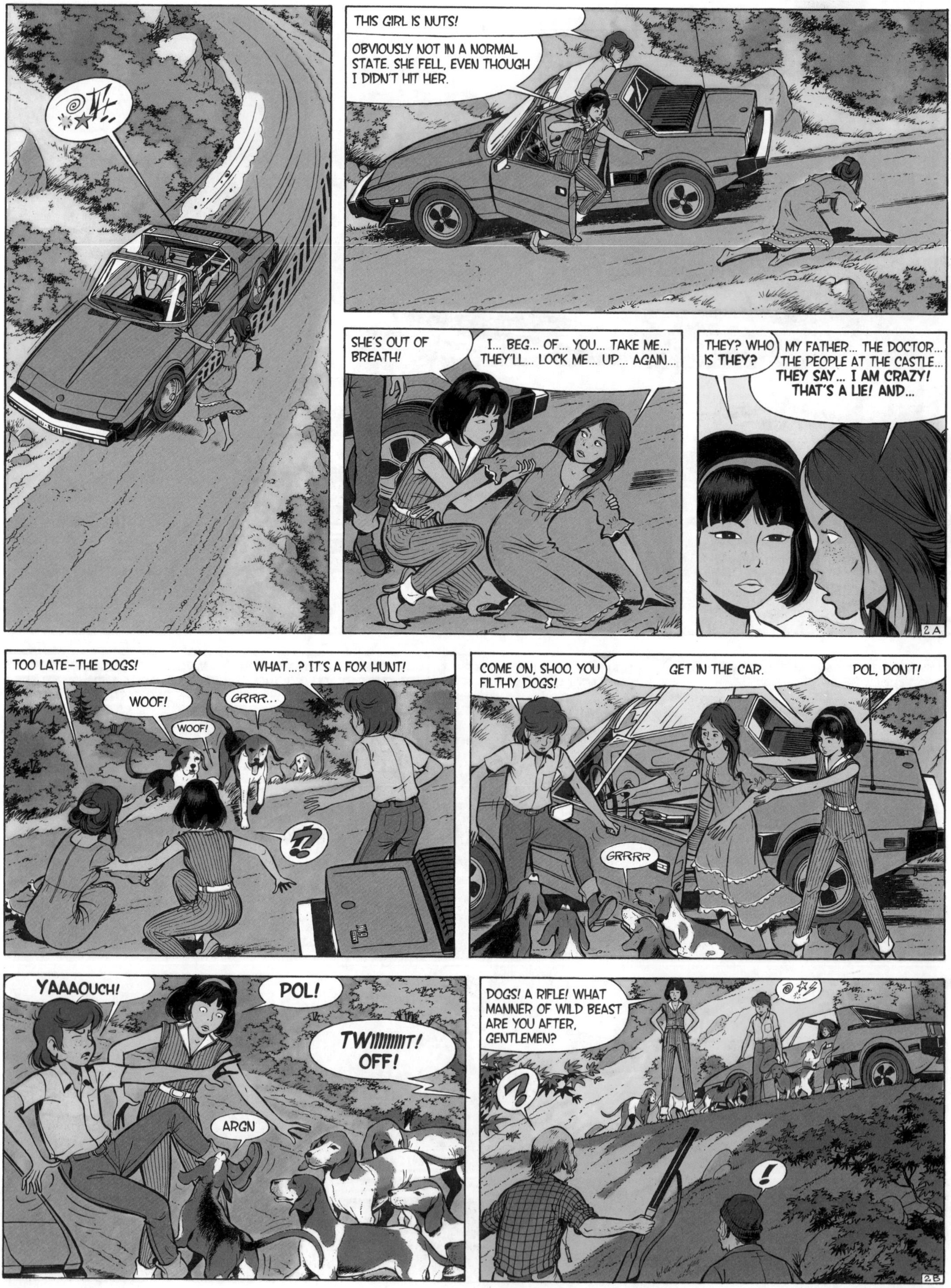
THIS GIRL IS NUTS!
OBVIOUSLY NOT IN A NORMAL STATE. SHE FELL, EVEN THOUGH I DIDN'T HIT HER.
SHE'S OUT OF BREATH!
I... BEG... OF... YOU... TAKE ME... THEY'LL... LOCK ME... UP... AGAIN...
THEY? WHO IS THEY?
MY FATHER... THE DOCTOR... THE PEOPLE AT THE CASTLE... THEY SAY... I AM CRAZY! THAT'S A LIE! AND...
2A
TOO LATE–THE DOGS!
WHAT...? IT'S A FOX HUNT!
WOOF!
WOOF!
GRRR...
COME ON, SHOO, YOU FILTHY DOGS!
GET IN THE CAR.
POL, DON'T!
GRRRR
YAAAOUCH!
POL!
TWIIIIIIIIT! OFF!
ARGN
DOGS! A RIFLE! WHAT MANNER OF WILD BEAST ARE YOU AFTER, GENTLEMEN?
2B

YOU MISUNDERSTAND, MISS. THE DOGS ARE TO FIND HER; THE RIFLE IS TO PROTECT HER **FROM HIM**!

WHO'S "HIM"??

YOU TALK TOO MUCH, JOHN.

TRUE. AND SIR WILLIAM OVER THERE DOES NOT APPRECIATE IT.

MY FATHER! IT WAS ALL FOR NOTHING...

YOUR DAUGHTER IS SAFE, SIR, BUT SHE NEEDS YOUR LOVE MORE THAN YOUR DOGS.

DO NOT BLAME A SORELY TESTED FATHER, MISS.

MY DAUGHTER CECILIA IS SUBJECT TO EPISODES, DURING WHICH SHE LOSES ALL REASON AND COMMITS THE WORST FOLLIES.

CALM DOWN!

I AM NOT CRAZY!

NO, CECILIA, JUST TEMPORARILY ILL... WE WILL TREAT YOU, AND YOU WILL GET BETTER.

YOU ARE KEEPING ME PRISONER! ALWAYS ALL ALONE IN THAT ROOM, NO FRIENDS... BUT NOT FOR MUCH LONGER!

MY MOTHER CAME AGAIN LAST NIGHT! AND SOON, **I SHALL LEAVE WITH HER!**

THEN WE MUST GO BACK TO THE CASTLE... OR SHE WILL NOT FIND YOU THERE.

VERY WELL, SIR, BUT WITH YOU GONE, WE REMAIN ALONE WITH OUR DOUBTS, AND OUR DAMAGE.

DAMAGE?

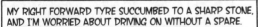

MY RIGHT FORWARD TYRE SUCCUMBED TO A SHARP STONE, AND I'M WORRIED ABOUT DRIVING ON WITHOUT A SPARE.

MY APOLOGIES; I DIDN'T KNOW. YOU WILL CHANGE YOUR TYRE, THEN JOIN US AT THE CASTLE. I WOULD BE HAPPY TO OFFER MY HOSPITALITY. I WILL SEND SOMEONE TO BRING UP A NEW TYRE...

... AND TOMORROW YOU WILL LEAVE WITH YOUR MIND AT EASE. FOR MY DAUGHTER'S EPISODES ARE BRIEF, AND YOU WILL FIND THAT IN BETWEEN THESE PAINFUL MOMENTS, SHE IS A CHARMING YOUNG LADY, MISS... ER...?

TSUNO. YOKO TSUNO.

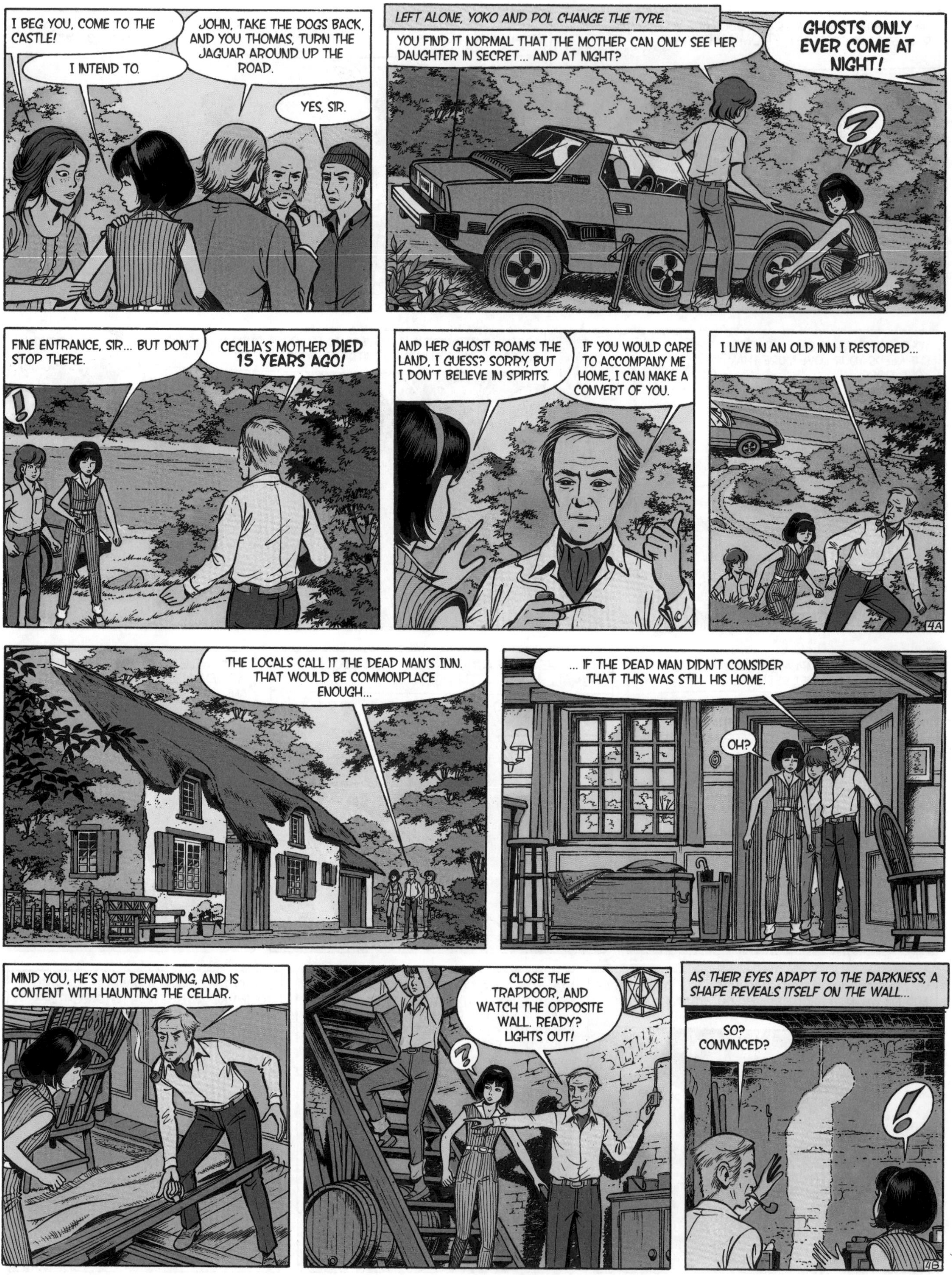

I BEG YOU, COME TO THE CASTLE!
I INTEND TO.
JOHN, TAKE THE DOGS BACK, AND YOU THOMAS, TURN THE JAGUAR AROUND UP THE ROAD.
YES, SIR.
LEFT ALONE, YOKO AND POL CHANGE THE TYRE.
YOU FIND IT NORMAL THAT THE MOTHER CAN ONLY SEE HER DAUGHTER IN SECRET... AND AT NIGHT?
GHOSTS ONLY EVER COME AT NIGHT!
FINE ENTRANCE, SIR... BUT DON'T STOP THERE.
CECILIA'S MOTHER DIED 15 YEARS AGO!
AND HER GHOST ROAMS THE LAND, I GUESS? SORRY, BUT I DON'T BELIEVE IN SPIRITS.
IF YOU WOULD CARE TO ACCOMPANY ME HOME, I CAN MAKE A CONVERT OF YOU.
I LIVE IN AN OLD INN I RESTORED...
4A
THE LOCALS CALL IT THE DEAD MAN'S INN. THAT WOULD BE COMMONPLACE ENOUGH...
... IF THE DEAD MAN DIDN'T CONSIDER THAT THIS WAS STILL HIS HOME.
OH?
MIND YOU, HE'S NOT DEMANDING, AND IS CONTENT WITH HAUNTING THE CELLAR.
CLOSE THE TRAPDOOR, AND WATCH THE OPPOSITE WALL. READY? LIGHTS OUT!
AS THEIR EYES ADAPT TO THE DARKNESS, A SHAPE REVEALS ITSELF ON THE WALL...
SO? CONVINCED?
4B

HOW DO YOU EXPLAIN THIS APPARITION?

SCIENTIFICALLY!

THIS POOR MAN HANGED HIMSELF FROM THIS BEAM, AFTER HAVING LIT THIS LANTERN HERE.

CLIC

HIS BODY CAST A SHADOW ON THE FRESHLY WHITEWASHED WALL OPPOSITE HIM... WHERE IT CAUSED A DIFFERENT CHEMICAL REACTION.

AND THIS "SHADOW" BEHAVES LIKE PHOSPHORESCENT MATTER.

EXACTLY! IT ABSORBS THE LIGHT, THEN RELEASES IT AS SOON AS YOU TURN IT OFF. THE PHENOMENON IS SHORT-LIVED... BUT LATELY IT HAS STARTED TO OCCUR BY ITSELF IN THE DARK!

WHAT DO YOU MEAN?

WE'LL HAVE TO COME BACK AND FILM THIS!

THAT A MADMAN IS BUSY MAKING **GHOSTS** APPEAR AROUND THESE PARTS... SEVERAL WITNESSES CONFIRM IT.

ANOTHER MADMAN?

YES. ALONG WITH GHOSTS, IT IS A LOCAL SPECIALTY. HMM. YOU CANNOT GO TO THE CASTLE UNAWARE OF THE SUCCESSIVE TRAGEDIES THAT HAVE TAKEN PLACE THERE. WHAT WOULD YOU LIKE TO DRINK?

A CUP OF TEA.

5A

CECILIA'S MOTHER WAS ONE OF THE PRETTIEST GIRLS AROUND THESE PARTS, AND HAD TWO SUITORS. SHE CHOSE SIR BRIAN FOR HIS WISDOM, AND REJECTED THE OTHER FOR HIS OCCULT PRACTICES.

ON THE WEDDING DAY, THIS WOULD-BE SORCERER CREATED A SCANDAL BY MAKING **A SORDID PROPHECY**: THE COUPLE WOULD DIE A VIOLENT DEATH, AND THEIR DAUGHTER WOULD NEVER REACH ADULTHOOD.

AND... IT CAME TRUE?

YES. SHORTLY AFTER CECILIA'S BIRTH, SIR BRIAN WAS KILLED IN A MYSTERIOUS ACCIDENT. HIS BROTHER, SIR WILLIAM, HASTILY CAME BACK FROM ABROAD TO HELP HIS SISTER-IN-LAW, WHOM HE MARRIED A YEAR LATER.

BUT IT WAS TOO LATE. WRACKED WITH GRIEF, LADY MARY WENT MAD AND, ON A STORMY NIGHT, LOST HER LIFE ON THE BACK OF A NERVOUS THOROUGHBRED.

GOOD GRIEF!

CECILIA WAS FIVE. SHE HAS JUST TURNED TWENTY AND, LIKE HER MOTHER, IS LOSING HER MIND. THE PREDICTION IS ACCOMPLISHED.

NOT QUITE. CECILIA IS STILL ALIVE!

5B

YES, BUT FOR HOW LONG? THAT MAN PROWLS AROUND THE CASTLE. SORCERY, BEWITCHMENT, ANYTHING GOES... BE CAREFUL, MISS. IF YOU COME ACROSS HIM, STAY WELL CLEAR: HE IS DANGEROUS!

THANK YOU FOR THE WARNING. BUT LET'S GO; I'M EAGER TO SEE CECILIA AGAIN.

SLIGHTLY PERPLEXED, YOKO AND POL ARE SOON BACK ON THEIR WAY TO THE CASTLE.

SO, DO YOU BELIEVE IN THIS CURSE?

WHAT I BELIEVE IS THAT SOME STRANGE PEOPLE ARE INTERESTED IN CECILIA.

SUCH AS THIS MAN IN BLACK WHO ACCOMPANIED SIR WILLIAM. PROBABLY THE DOCTOR SHE SPOKE OF.

YES. SINISTER CHARACTER!

THE FIRST THING TO DO IS TO CALL VIC, WHO'S WAITING FOR US AT INVERNESS, AND WARN HIM OF OUR "MISHAP."

OH! BEAUTIFUL STAGE FOR A TRAGEDY!

WELCOME TO LOCH CASTLE, MISS TSUNO! YOU SEEM TO HAVE TAKEN SOME TIME TO CHANGE THIS TYRE... ANY PROBLEMS?

NO, SIR. WE TALKED A BIT TO GIVE MISS CECILIA TIME TO REGAIN HER COMPOSURE. HOW IS SHE?

BETTER. DONALD, TAKE THESE YOUNG PEOPLE'S LUGGAGE TO THEIR ROOMS.

HELP ME PUT THE HARDTOP BACK FIRST.

MY APOLOGIES, BUT I COULD NOT GIVE YOU ADJOINING ROOMS.

IT DOESN'T MATTER, SIR.

WOW. NICE COUNTRY HOUSE!

THE LADY'S SUITCASE IS IN HER ROOM, SIR.

VERY GOOD, DONALD. PLEASE TAKE THE YOUNG MAN TO HIS.

AH, OF COURSE, IT'S THE ATTIC FOR ME AGAIN!

I DECIDED TO PUT YOU UP IN THE ANNEX, NEXT TO CECILIA'S ROOM.

THANK YOU FOR THIS SIGN OF TRUST.

MAKE YOURSELF AT HOME. IF YOU NEED ANYTHING, RING.

OH!

IT'S... FIT FOR A PRINCESS!

FIT FOR YOU! AS SOON AS IT WILL BE CONVENIENT, JOIN ME IN THE SITTING-ROOM.

THE VIEW OVER THE LAKE IS GLORIOUS... FIRST, TO FRESHEN UP, AND CHANGE CLOTHES. THEN I WILL GO ASK SIR WILLIAM A FEW QUESTIONS...

9

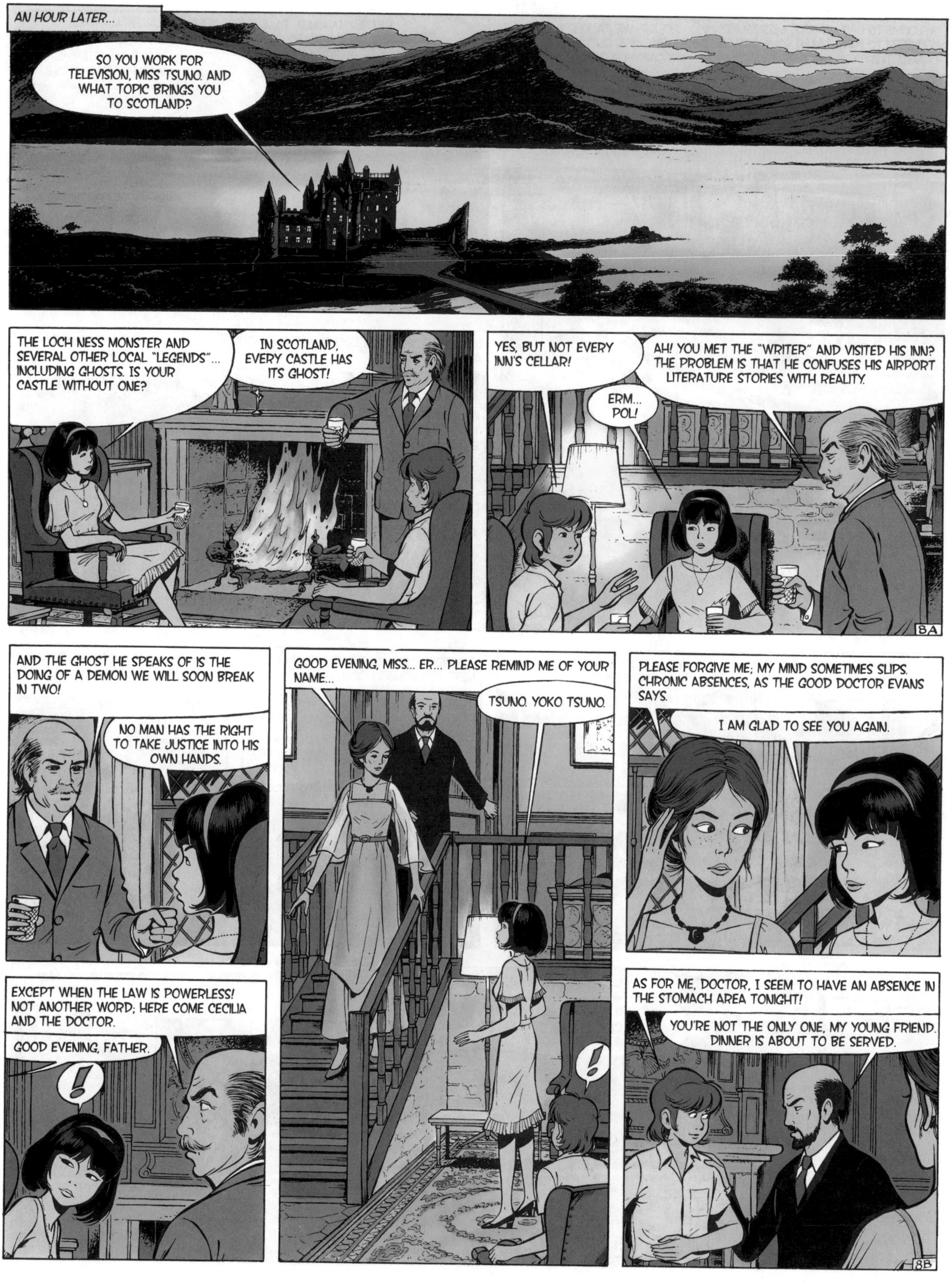
AN HOUR LATER...
SO YOU WORK FOR TELEVISION, MISS TSUNO. AND WHAT TOPIC BRINGS YOU TO SCOTLAND?
THE LOCH NESS MONSTER AND SEVERAL OTHER LOCAL "LEGENDS"... INCLUDING GHOSTS. IS YOUR CASTLE WITHOUT ONE?
IN SCOTLAND, EVERY CASTLE HAS ITS GHOST!
YES, BUT NOT EVERY INN'S CELLAR!
AH! YOU MET THE "WRITER" AND VISITED HIS INN? THE PROBLEM IS THAT HE CONFUSES HIS AIRPORT LITERATURE STORIES WITH REALITY.
ERM... POL!
8A
AND THE GHOST HE SPEAKS OF IS THE DOING OF A DEMON WE WILL SOON BREAK IN TWO!
NO MAN HAS THE RIGHT TO TAKE JUSTICE INTO HIS OWN HANDS.
EXCEPT WHEN THE LAW IS POWERLESS! NOT ANOTHER WORD; HERE COME CECILIA AND THE DOCTOR.
GOOD EVENING, FATHER.
!
GOOD EVENING, MISS... ER... PLEASE REMIND ME OF YOUR NAME...
TSUNO. YOKO TSUNO.
!
PLEASE FORGIVE ME; MY MIND SOMETIMES SLIPS. CHRONIC ABSENCES, AS THE GOOD DOCTOR EVANS SAYS.
I AM GLAD TO SEE YOU AGAIN.
AS FOR ME, DOCTOR, I SEEM TO HAVE AN ABSENCE IN THE STOMACH AREA TONIGHT!
YOU'RE NOT THE ONLY ONE, MY YOUNG FRIEND. DINNER IS ABOUT TO BE SERVED.
8B

A LITTLE MORE ICE CREAM, MISS?

NO, THANK YOU.

DRIFT ALONG THIS WAY, MY GOOD MAN; I'LL TAKE IT!

CECILIA IS SULKING.

YOU ARE A FIRST-CLASS GUEST, MR POL.

I DO APOLOGISE, BUT I DON'T HAVE MUCH APPETITE TONIGHT.

COULD IT BE THAT THE COMPASSION YOU FEEL FOR ME ROBBED YOU OF IT?

IT WOULD BE A MISTAKE, BECAUSE I DO NOT CARE FOR PEOPLE'S PITY!

CECILIA!

I DID NOT COME OUT OF PITY, BUT IN FRIENDSHIP... AND SINCE IT UPSETS YOU, ALLOW ME TO RETIRE TO MY ROOM...

... SO I CAN KEEP INTACT THE MEMORY OF THE CECILIA I MET UP THERE!

PLEASE FORGIVE ME; I DID NOT MEAN TO HURT YOU.

COME, MISS, I'LL TAKE YOU BACK TO YOUR ROOM.

LEAVE ME!

I WAS HORRIBLE, WASN'T I?

MERELY TOUCHY. CECILIA HATES FOR PEOPLE TO MENTION HER PERSONALITY SWITCHES.

SHE CAN'T FORGIVE THAT YOU SAW HER IN HER MADNESS... WHAT'S MORE, SHE'S UNDER THE EFFECT OF THE SEDATIVES I GAVE HER.

I SHOULD HAVE THOUGHT OF THAT.

AH! ANOTHER THING... AT NIGHT, THE LIGHTS SOMETIMES GO DIM FROM LACK OF POWER. GOOD NIGHT, MISS.

GOOD NIGHT.

SHE DID EVERYTHING SHE COULD TO VEX ME, AND I STUPIDLY TOOK THE BAIT. THAT ICE CREAM MADE ME THIRSTY... AH! A WATER JUG.

CECILIA IS DISCONCERTING... WARM IN HER MADNESS, ICY IN HER LUCIDITY.

OH! THE GLASS!

STILL IN ONE PIECE. BUT THE BEDSIDE RUG IS SOAKED... I'M A FAILURE AT EVERYTHING TONIGHT!

I'D BETTER GO TO SLEEP. MAYBE TOMORROW WILL BRING ME CECILIA'S SMILE...

MIDNIGHT IS CLOSE. IN THE CASTLE, EVERYTHING IS ASLEEP... ALMOST.

YOU'RE STICKING WITH THE PROGRAM DESPITE... THE JAPANESE GIRL?

YES! "HE" HAS NEVER BEEN MORE PREPARED TO TAKE THE BAIT.

STILL, IT'S RISKY.

A CALCULATED RISK, DEAR FELLOW. AND NOW, IT IS TIME TO BEGIN.

IN HER ROOM, HER MIND RESTLESS, SLEEP ELUDES YOKO.

I AM TOO WORKED UP; THAT'S GOING TO MEAN A SLEEPLESS NIGHT.

SOMEONE'S OPENING MY DOOR!

CLICK CRRRR

... BUT SUFFICIENT TO REVEAL A DARK SILHOUETTE.

?!

WHO... WHO ARE YOU? WHAT DO YOU WANT FROM ME?

COME! COME!

WHO... WHO'S THERE?

COME!

YOKO FEELS ALONG THE WALL FOR THE LIGHT SWITCH... BUT WHEN SHE FINDS IT, ALL SHE GETS IS A DIM GLOW...

THE POWER...

CLICK

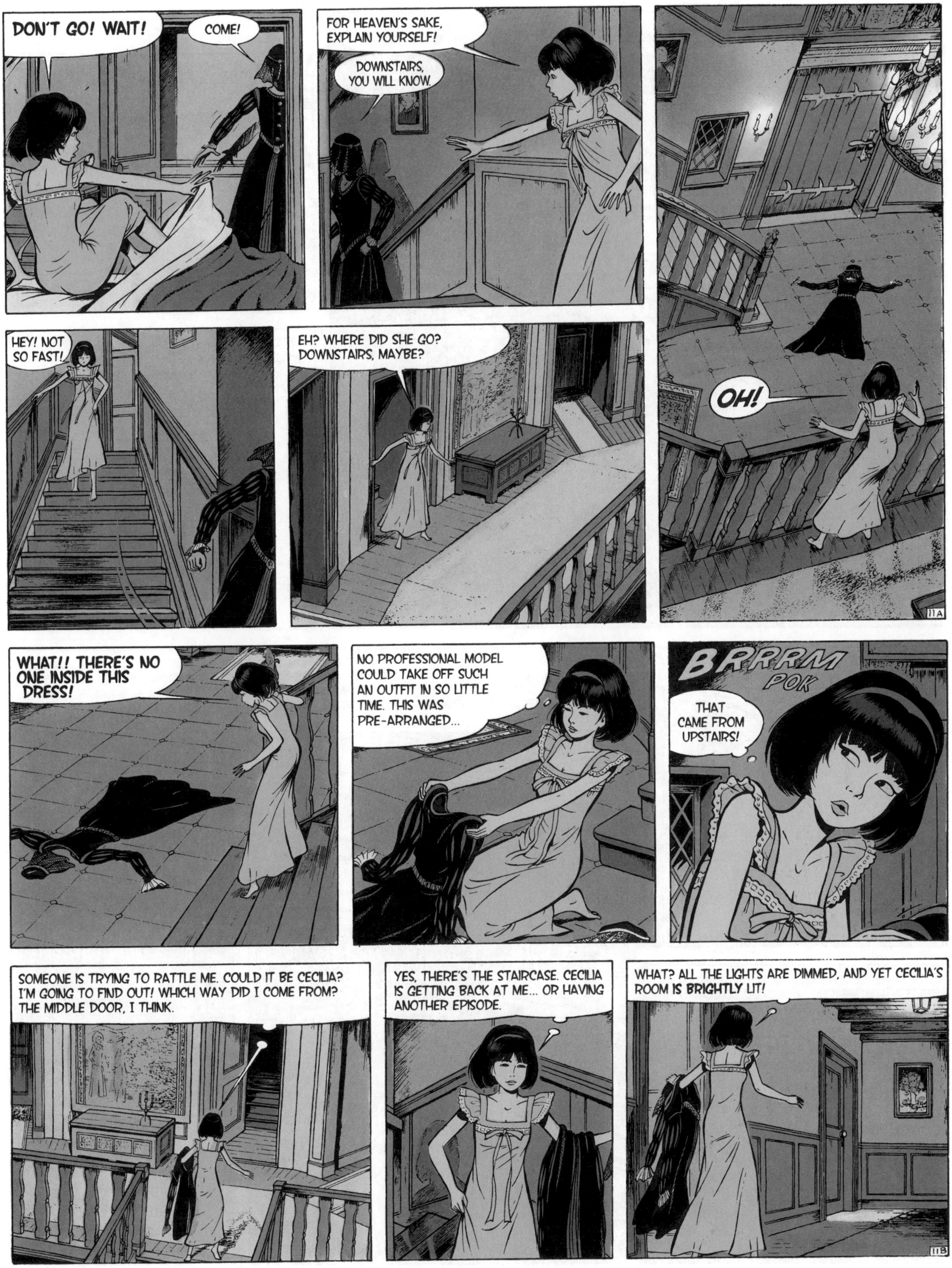
DON'T GO! WAIT!
COME!
FOR HEAVEN'S SAKE, EXPLAIN YOURSELF!
DOWNSTAIRS, YOU WILL KNOW.
HEY! NOT SO FAST!
EH? WHERE DID SHE GO? DOWNSTAIRS, MAYBE?
OH!
11A
WHAT!! THERE'S NO ONE INSIDE THIS DRESS!
NO PROFESSIONAL MODEL COULD TAKE OFF SUCH AN OUTFIT IN SO LITTLE TIME. THIS WAS PRE-ARRANGED...
BRRRM
POK
THAT CAME FROM UPSTAIRS!
SOMEONE IS TRYING TO RATTLE ME. COULD IT BE CECILIA? I'M GOING TO FIND OUT! WHICH WAY DID I COME FROM? THE MIDDLE DOOR, I THINK.
YES, THERE'S THE STAIRCASE. CECILIA IS GETTING BACK AT ME... OR HAVING ANOTHER EPISODE.
WHAT? ALL THE LIGHTS ARE DIMMED, AND YET CECILIA'S ROOM IS BRIGHTLY LIT!
11B

YOKO HAS WALKED TO CECILIA'S DOOR...

LOCKED. AND THE KEY IS ON THE OUTSIDE...

SHE'S PAINTING...

... BY THE LIGHT OF OIL LAMPS!

YOU! I'D GIVEN UP HOPE! WHAT? THAT'S ONE OF MY MOTHER'S DRESSES YOU'RE HOLDING THERE!

IN FACT, IT'S A COPY OF A PERIOD DRESS SHE LOVED TO WEAR...

IT'S ALL THAT'S LEFT OF THE STRANGER I FOLLOWED INTO THE HALL... WHERE SHE VANISHED!

OH?

OH! BUT...

THIS DRESS WAS KEPT HERE, AND IT'S GONE.

SOMEONE BORROWED IT FROM YOU.

LET'S SAY... TOOK IT BACK. BECAUSE IT IS MY MOTHER WHO DREW YOU TO ME.

I'D LIKE TO BELIEVE THAT!

MY MOTHER COULD PAINT FLOWERS ADMIRABLY... BETTER THAN ME. STILL, I DECIDED TO COMPLETE THIS ONE SHE HAD LEFT UNFINISHED.

EXCELLENT IDEA.

MY FATHER HAD BEEN SUGGESTING IT FOR A LONG TIME. ONE MORNING, I FOUND A FLOWER I'D SKETCHED THE DAY BEFORE, MASTERFULLY COMPLETED. AFTER THE SAME THING HAD HAPPENED SEVERAL TIMES, ONE NIGHT I PRETENDED TO SLEEP... AND I SAW HER!

YOUR MOTHER?

YES, YOKO, MY MOTHER! WEARING HER WEDDING DRESS, JUST LIKE IN THIS PORTRAIT. SHE WAS THERE, ETHEREAL, NEXT TO THE EASEL...

WHAT DID YOU DO?

FACED WITH MY MOTHER'S GHOST, I TOOK FRIGHT AND SCREAMED. SHE VANISHED IMMEDIATELY!

DID THIS GHOST EVER COME BACK?

YES, BUT NO LONGER IN MY BEDROOM...

SOME NIGHTS SHE APPEARS TO ME ON THE WALL WALK, THERE, NEAR THE OLD TOWER.

AND YOU'VE NEVER BEEN ABLE TO GET NEAR HER?

NO, BECAUSE I AM LOCKED IN HERE. BUT, THANKS TO YOU TONIGHT, WE'LL BE ABLE TO GO TO HER!

ASSUMING SHE COMES.

SHE WILL COME; THERE IS NO MIST TONIGHT.

IT'S CHILLY, THOUGH. YOU WOULDN'T HAVE A DRESS FOR ME?

CHOOSE ONE FROM THE WARDROBE; WE'RE THE SAME SIZE.

SO MANY PRETTY DRESSES!

THEY ARE... MY MOTHER'S. MY FATHER LIKES ME TO WEAR THEM... IT'S HIS WAY OF BRINGING A GHOST BACK TO LIFE.

I LIKE THIS ONE.

YOUR GHOST, I'M SURE, IS NOTHING BUT A HOAX.

WE'LL DIM THE LIGHTS AND WAIT FOR HER.

AN HOUR HAS PASSED.
YOU BELIEVE, AS THE OTHERS DO, THAT I AM CRAZY AND SEEING THINGS?

ER... I DIDN'T SAY THAT!

THEN, YOKO, WE SHALL BOTH BE SEEING THINGS. LOOK, DOWN THERE!

SO? DO YOU BELIEVE ME, NOW?

WELL, I NEVER!

ON THE WALL WALK, A GLOWING FIGURE STANDS, ARMS EXTENDED TOWARDS THE STUNNED YOUNG WOMEN.

IT'S HER ALL RIGHT, JUST LIKE THE PORTRAIT!

THAT STILL DOESN'T PROVE SHE'S A GHOST...

THAT'S EASY. MY DOOR IS OPEN. THERE'S NOTHING TO STOP US FROM JOINING HER...

ALL RIGHT, BUT I'M GOING ALONE.

STAY IN SIGHT AT THE WINDOW. IF THIS IS A HOAX, I'LL SOON INTRODUCE YOU TO ITS AUTHOR.

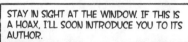

BUT AS YOKO NEARS THE DOOR...

THE DOOR OPENED BY ITSELF!

CLICK

RUNNING HARD...

MAYBE IT WAS A COINCIDENCE...

... YOKO REACHES THE ENTRANCE HALL.

NO! IT'S AN INVITATION; THE FRONT DOOR IS OPEN TOO!

WHOA! SHE ALMOST GOT AWAY FROM ME!

YOKO!

WOW, SHE'S FAST!

CECILIA, FOLLOW!

BUT BY THE CASTLE'S OUTBUILDINGS...

SHE PICKED UP SPEED AGAIN!

THE DOGS? WEIRD. OH, WHERE DID SHE GO?

WOOF!

WOOF!

WOOF!

THERE SHE IS... WHAT? IT LOOKS LIKE SHE'S WAITING FOR ME!!

BUT AS YOKO DRAWS CLOSER, THE "GHOST" RESUMES HER GRACEFUL RUNNING...

QUICKLY CECILIA, SHE'S OFF AGAIN!

WAIT!

17

I'M... EXHAUSTED... KEEP GOING... ALONE!

IN ANY CASE, I KNOW WHERE SHE'S GOING.

AND YOKO WILL HAVE A BIG SURPRISE!

THE RUINS OF AN ABBEY... SHE MUST KNOW THEM WELL. SHE'LL LOSE ME IN THERE.

RUNNING STRAIGHT AS AN ARROW, THE "GHOST" ENTERS THE REMAINS OF A CHAPEL...

UNLESS SHE CAN WALK THROUGH WALLS, SHE'LL HAVE TO CHANGE DIRECTION.

... AT THE BACK OF WHICH SHE SUDDENLY TURNS BACK, HOLDING OUT HER HANDS TO AN ASTONISHED YOKO.

UNEXPECTED CHANGE OF HEART... THIS DOESN'T FEEL RIGHT!

18

IF I TRY A FRONTAL ASSAULT, SHE'LL FLY OUT THE DOOR ON THE RIGHT...

BUT IF I CUT OFF THAT EXIT, SHE CAN ONLY RETRACE HER STEPS...

... TOWARDS CECILIA!

WITHOUT GAINING ON ME!

SHE HASN'T MOVED AN INCH. THIS TIME...

I'VE GOT HER!

HAAAA

I WENT STRAIGHT...

... THROUGH!

THEN... IT CAN ONLY BE... HOW DID I NOT THINK OF THAT EARLIER?

19

HEY! SHE'S FADING!...

INDEED, AS THE "GHOST" LOSES ITS LUMINOSITY, IT BECOMES MORE AND MORE TRANSPARENT...

IT'S SCIENTIFICALLY WONDERFUL...

... AND A DIABOLICAL IDEA.

... AND SOON VANISHES.

BUT WHOSE? AND TO WHAT END? FINISHED... GONE!

YOKO?

SHE'S ON THE RIGHT TRACK... BUT WILL SHE GO ALL THE WAY TO THE TRUTH?

CECILIA? WHERE ARE YOU?

THIS WAY, YOKO! SHE GOT AWAY FROM YOU, DIDN'T SHE?

SHE DID, I'M AFRAID... HEY! IT'S A GRAVEYARD!

YOU FRIGHTENED HER... SHE'S TRYING TO GO BACK TO WHERE SHE CAME FROM.

AND WHERE DO YOU FIGURE SHE COMES FROM?

FROM **HER GRAVE!** AROUND WHICH AN EVIL HAND HAS ERECTED AN IMPASSABLE RING.

YOU MEAN SOMEONE IS TRYING TO PREVENT HER FROM GETTING BACK INSIDE HER GRAVE?

YES, AND FORCE HER TO WANDER AMONG US FOREVER. DON'T TOUCH IT—IT'S DANGEROUS!

MOVING A FEW STONES IS NOTHING DANGE...

SUDDENLY THE LIFTED STONE BURSTS INTO FLAMES...

HAAAAA

THE BOTTOM WAS COVERED IN A SUBSTANCE THAT BURNS ON CONTACT WITH THE AIR; AND THE STONE RESTED ON A PLASTIC BAG FULL OF WATER. AN ILLUSIONIST'S TRICK.

BUT THIS ONE IS VERY SMART. ONLY ONE STONE WAS BOOBY-TRAPPED. HOW COULD HE HAVE KNOWN WHICH ONE WOULD BE LIFTED?

MAC NAB IS A MADMAN!

HIS SPELLS DESTROYED MY PARENTS' HAPPINESS, AND NOW HE IS HARASSING MY MOTHER IN HER ETERNAL REST.

DID HE DO ANYTHING AGAINST YOU?

THAT WOULD BE DIFFICULT FOR HIM: I AM WELL PROTECTED. I'M MORE WORRIED ABOUT MY MOTHER'S GHOST... WHAT DOES SHE WANT TO TELL ME? SHE'LL BE BACK, AND I'LL KNOW.

LISTEN!

THE DOGS!

THEY'RE COMING TO BRING US BACK...

WOOF!

WOOF!

EASY! CALM DOWN!

HEY! HE'S GOING TO TEAR MY DRESS!

SHE'S OVER HERE, SIR WILLIAM! WITH MISS TSUNO!

MISS TSUNO! ARE YOU NOW ENCOURAGING MY DAUGHTER'S ESCAPADES?

LET'S SAY I'M TRYING TO UNDER-STAND HER.

THERE'S NOTHING TO UNDERSTAND. MAC NAB IS A SCOUNDREL WHO... WHAT THE...?

ROSES! ROSES AGAIN! CURSE YOU! ONE DAY I WILL MAKE YOU EAT THEM!

SIR!

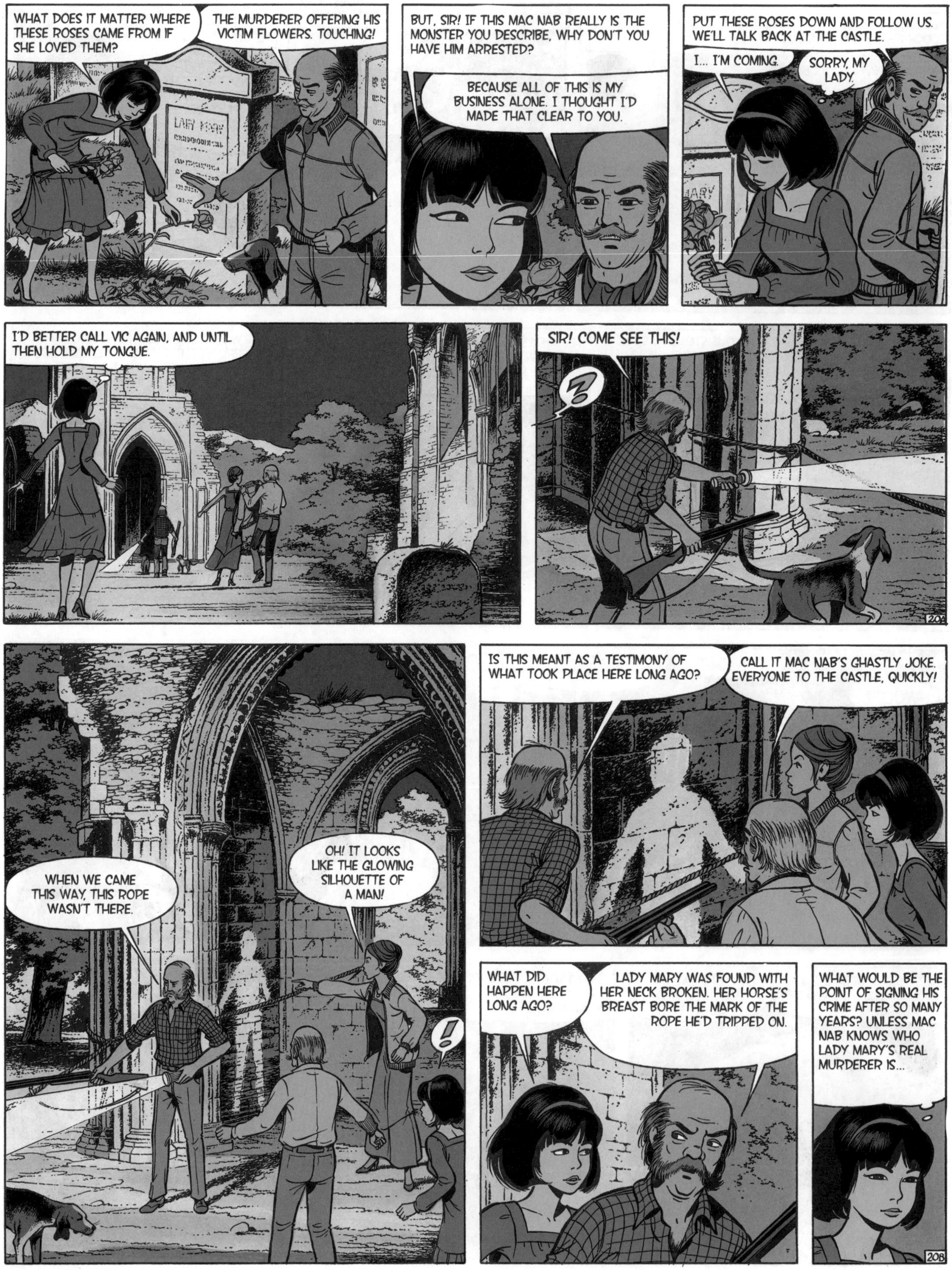

WHAT DOES IT MATTER WHERE THESE ROSES CAME FROM IF SHE LOVED THEM?
THE MURDERER OFFERING HIS VICTIM FLOWERS. TOUCHING!
BUT, SIR! IF THIS MAC NAB REALLY IS THE MONSTER YOU DESCRIBE, WHY DON'T YOU HAVE HIM ARRESTED?
BECAUSE ALL OF THIS IS MY BUSINESS ALONE. I THOUGHT I'D MADE THAT CLEAR TO YOU.
PUT THESE ROSES DOWN AND FOLLOW US. WE'LL TALK BACK AT THE CASTLE.
I... I'M COMING.
SORRY, MY LADY.
I'D BETTER CALL VIC AGAIN, AND UNTIL THEN HOLD MY TONGUE.
SIR! COME SEE THIS!
20A
WHEN WE CAME THIS WAY, THIS ROPE WASN'T THERE.
OH! IT LOOKS LIKE THE GLOWING SILHOUETTE OF A MAN!
!
IS THIS MEANT AS A TESTIMONY OF WHAT TOOK PLACE HERE LONG AGO?
CALL IT MAC NAB'S GHASTLY JOKE. EVERYONE TO THE CASTLE, QUICKLY!
WHAT DID HAPPEN HERE LONG AGO?
LADY MARY WAS FOUND WITH HER NECK BROKEN. HER HORSE'S BREAST BORE THE MARK OF THE ROPE HE'D TRIPPED ON.
WHAT WOULD BE THE POINT OF SIGNING HIS CRIME AFTER SO MANY YEARS? UNLESS MAC NAB KNOWS WHO LADY MARY'S REAL MURDERER IS...
20B

THE SMALL GROUP WAS SOON BACK AT THE CASTLE.

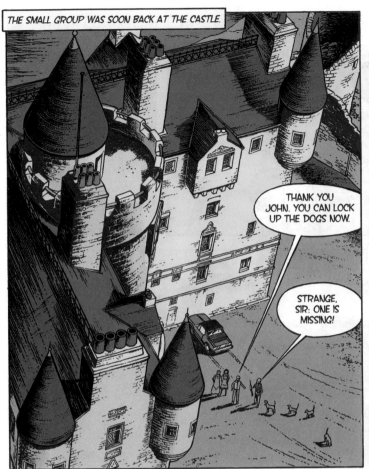

THANK YOU JOHN. YOU CAN LOCK UP THE DOGS NOW.

STRANGE, SIR: ONE IS MISSING!

OH? MISS TSUNO WAS INVOLVED?

YES, BUT FORTUNATELY EVERYTHING TURNED OUT FINE. MEET US IN CECILIA'S ROOM.

ACHOO!

I CAUGHT A COLD...

WHILE I MAKE HER TALK, MAKE SURE EVERYTHING IS... SYNCHRONIZED.

COUNT ON ME.

PECULIAR PLACE, THIS CASTLE. THE LIGHTS COME BACK WHEN THE GHOSTS LEAVE.

HALF AN HOUR LATER, IN CECILIA'S ROOM.

... AND YOU FOLLOWED THIS GHOST INTO THE CHAPEL?

NOT RIGHT AWAY. I... I'D LOST A SHOE... AND WHEN I WENT INSIDE, THE CHAPEL WAS EMPTY...

I'M A BAD LIAR.

I WAS CHECKING THE AREA WHEN CECILIA CALLED ME TO THE GRAVEYARD.

IN THE HALL, WHEN YOU FOUND THE DRESS, DID YOU NOTICE ANYTHING OUT OF PLACE?

EVERYTHING WAS OUT OF PLACE... THE BLACK LADY... THE EMPTY DRESS... AND THEN... WAIT... YES! A NOISE!

... IT WAS LIKE SOMETHING HEAVY ROLLING.

REALLY? HOW STRANGE...

HERE'S SOMETHING EFFECTIVE AGAINST BOTH NERVES AND COLD.

23

WHAT IS IT?

HERBAL TEA. SO YOU CAN WAKE UP TOMORROW WITH A CLEAR AND UNWORRIED MIND.

DOES WONDERS FOR YOUR SLEEP?

REFRESHING, ISN'T IT?

HERBAL TEA? OR DRUG? I DON'T HAVE A CHOICE...

MMMM

WELL! TO GAUGE THE EFFECT OF YOUR HERBAL TEA, I SHALL GO TO BED.

SEE YOU TOMORROW, CECILIA.

GOOD NIGHT, YOKO, AND... THANK YOU!

AND A SHORT WHILE LATER...

THE DOG RIPPED THE BOTTOM OF MY DRESS...

OH? WHAT IS THIS?

IT LOOKS LIKE A LEAD RIBBON, LIKE TAILORS USE TO WEIGH DOWN LIGHT DRESSES... NO, THAT'S NOT LEAD!

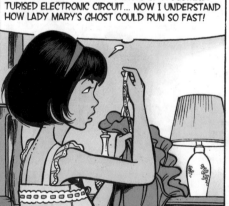

THERE ARE ALL THE COMPONENTS OF A SUBMINIA-TURISED ELECTRONIC CIRCUIT... NOW I UNDERSTAND HOW LADY MARY'S GHOST COULD RUN SO FAST!

OH? THE RUG I DROPPED A GLASS ON IS ALREADY DRY!

THEY MUST HAVE REPLACED IT.

OOOH, I FEEL DIZZY... PROBABLY THE DOCTOR'S HERBAL TEA.

AND SOON...

TOO STRONG... FOR TEA... IT WAS... DRUGGED...

MEANWHILE, IN ANOTHER ROOM OF THE CASTLE...

STOP FRETTING. IN HALF AN HOUR YOU'LL BE ABLE TO FIRE A CANNON WITHOUT WAKING HER UP.

ALL RIGHT! BUT TOMORROW MORNING, SHE HAS TO GO!

THE CASTLE IS STILL DAMP FROM AN EARLY MORNING MIST WHEN...

MY, DID I SLEEP WELL!

THE DOCTOR'S "DRUG" WAS AN EXCELLENT TEA!

OH? ROSES! THEY WERE LEFT WHILE I WAS ASLEEP. WHAT'S THIS? A NOTE!

?

TWO ROSES ON A BRANCH... THE FIRST WITHERED AND DIED, THE SECOND COULDN'T SURVIVE...

HOW VERY CRYPTIC.

TWO ROSES ON A BRANCH... THERE'S A REFERENCE THERE, BUT TO WHAT?

MAYBE CECILIA CAN MAKE MORE OUT OF IT...

HEY!

SPLOTSH!

THE BEDSIDE RUG IS SOAKED AGAIN... BUT LAST NIGHT IT WASN'T...

AH, THE DRESS! THE RIBBON!

BUT EVEN THOUGH YOKO SCRUTINIZES THE DRESS HEM...

NO SIGN OF A TEAR... AND THE RIBBON VANISHED, AS IF I HAD DREAMED IT.

UNLESS... I MUST CHECK CECILIA'S ROOM.

25

SOON YOKO IS KNOCKING ON CECILIA'S DOOR.

NO ANSWER. IS SHE STILL ASLEEP?

KNOCK KNOCK

CECILIA?

NO ONE. THE WARDROBE...

THE DRESS REALLY IS MISSING. THERE GOES MY THEORY...

SOMEONE IS COMING!

YOUR MISCONDUCT LAST NIGHT...

... FORCES ME TO LOCK YOU UP IN YOUR ROOM UNTIL THE JAPANESE GIRL IS GONE!

I CAN'T TAKE MUCH MORE OF THIS; THEY'RE DRIVING ME INSANE!

CLAP

CLICK

24A

CECILIA HAS COLLAPSED UPON HER BED.

OH, MOMMY... WHY DID YOU LEAVE ME SO SOON?

ERM...

CECILIA... I'D LIKE TO HELP YOU.

YOU! WHAT ARE YOU DOING HERE?

I WAS RETURNING YOUR DRESS. WHEN I HEARD THE DOCTOR, I HID.

IT'S LUCKY HE DIDN'T SEE YOU... YOU CANNOT STAY HERE, YOKO!

LITTLE CHOICE DO I HAVE! THE DOCTOR LOCKED THE DOOR, AND I DON'T REALLY SEE MYSELF...

... JUMPING OUT THE WIN...

OH!

?

24B

THE WALL WALK! THE TOWER!

WHAT IS IT? YOU'VE GONE ALL WHITE!

ER... DIZZY SPELL... IT'S HIGH!

I'LL LET YOU OUT THROUGH THE SECRET PASSAGE.

A SECRET PASSAGE?

BUT AS SHE WALKS PAST THE PAINTING, YOKO QUICKLY BRUSHES HER FINGERS AGAINST IT.

NOW I'M SURE; **THIS IS NOT THE ROOM** I WAS IN LAST NIGHT.

NO ONE KNOWS I'M AWARE OF THIS PASSAGEWAY'S EXISTENCE.

AND AFTER CLOSING THE PANEL...

WHERE ARE WE?

BETWEEN TWO WALLS.

STEP ON THE BEAMS!

WE GO UP THIS WAY.

AND THAT WAY?

AN OLD TUNNEL THAT LEADS TO THE ABBEY. FORBIDDEN. DANGEROUS!

THIS STAIR-WAY LEADS TO THE ARMS ROOM.

THE YOUNG WOMEN SOON COME OUT INSIDE THE ARMS ROOM.

NO ONE AROUND. QUICKLY!

WHAT ARE YOU LOOKING AT THERE?

THE OPENING MECHANISM.

JUST PRESS TO UNLOCK.

I FORBID YOU TO RETRACE YOUR STEPS THAT WAY TO SEE ME AGAIN BEFORE YOU LEAVE! UNDERSTOOD?

ER... UNDERSTOOD.

26A

AS THE PANEL CLOSES AFTER CECILIA...

UNDERSTOOD, BUT NO PROMISES MADE!

KLAK

OH! DON... DONALD! YOU STARTLED ME!

MISS TSUNO! MIGHT YOU BE LOOKING FOR POOR MR POL'S ROOM?

ERM, YES, THAT'S IT. WHY POOR?

BECAUSE HE'S SUFFERING FROM TERRIBLE INDIGESTION! I WILL TAKE YOU THERE.

AND SOON AFTER...

I'M ABOUT TO DIE... AND HE WANTS TO STICK A NEEDLE IN ME!

IT'S TO RELIEVE YOUR NAUSEA.

YOU HAVE TO ADMIT, YOU RATHER BROUGHT IT ON YOURSELF! THREE SERVINGS OF ICE CREAM, TWO SLICES OF CAKE, ICE-COLD BEER... AND I'LL SPARE YOU WHAT FOLLOWED!

DON'T WORRY. HE'LL BE ON HIS FEET BY NOON.

BY... NOON? I'LL LET VIC KNOW.

SAD FOR POL, BUT A GODSEND FOR ME.

26B

HALF AN HOUR LATER...

HELLO? VIC? YES, IT'S ME... SLIGHT PROBLEM: POL IS SICK...

NO, NOTHING SERIOUS... BUT I'D LIKE YOU TO COME HERE, YES... RENT A CAR; I'LL EXPLAIN. BE QUICK!

HAVING GONE BACK TO HER ROOM, YOKO IS GEARING UP...

I'LL BORROW A CANDLESTICK... THEN I'LL HAVE TO FIND SOME MATCHES.

AND SHORTLY AFTER, IN THE ARMS ROOM...

YOU JUST PUSH ON THE MOLDING...

AND NOW, LET'S HAVE A LOOK AT THIS FORBIDDEN TUNNEL.

IT GOES WELL BELOW THE CELLARS.

SO MUCH DAMP! I MUST BE UNDER THE RIVER.

CECILIA WASN'T LYING: THIS PLACE IS DANGEROUS.

A FEW MINUTES LATER...

THIS CORRIDOR SEEMS ENDLESS, AND SOME PARTS ARE READY TO COLLAPSE.

AH! I'M ALMOST THERE!

29

THERE'S NO DOUBT: I'M IN A CRYPT UNDER THE ABBEY... AND THAT OVER THERE IS DAYLIGHT.

OH! SERIOUS COLLAPSE!

A STAIRCASE!

BUT? THAT'S A DOG DOWN THERE! COULD IT BE THE ONE THAT WENT MISSING LAST NIGHT?

STONE DEAD... HE MUST HAVE FALLEN FROM GROUND LEVEL. I'D BETTER GO AND SEE; THE STAIRCASE WILL LEAD ME THERE.

YES! IT'S THE CHAPEL I FOUND LAST NIGHT. IF I HADN'T STOPPED IN TIME, I WOULD HAVE STEPPED OFF INTO THIS HOLE WITHOUT EVER SEEING IT. THE DOG WAS FOLLOWING IN MY TRACKS AND WASN'T SO LUCKY, AND...

THAT MEANS...? CECILIA... THE SPECTRE... THE PREY! THE GHOST! OH! THE HORRIBLE CRIME!

SOON...

THESE STAIRS JUST KEEP GOING...

PHEW, AT LAST! OH? I RECOGNISE THIS PLACE.

30

IF WHAT I HAVE IN MIND IS TRUE, I AM THE KEEPER OF A SECRET THAT COULD COST ME MY LIFE.

I'LL HAVE TO EMPLOY EXCELLENT ACTING SKILLS TO AVOID RAISING SUSPICION. LET'S NOT STICK AROUND HERE.

I'LL HIDE THIS CANDLESTICK AND GET BACK TO THE CASTLE BY ANOTHER ROUTE... OH? LOOKS LIKE MORE RUINS UP THERE!

PROBABLY THE REMAINS OF THE SECOND CASTLE, WHERE THE MANSERVANT SAYS THIS MYSTERIOUS MAC NAB LIVES.

AND SOON...

OH! GLOOMY PLACE!

SO THIS IS THE SORCERER'S LAIR. BUT... IS HE TRULY ONE?

KNOCK KNOCK KNOCK

ANYBODY HERE?

APPARENTLY NOT.

31

MMH! A TALENTED COOK, THIS MAC NAB. A TORTURE FOR MY EMPTY STOMACH.

SO, THIS IS HIS WORKSHOP...

EYE OF NEWT... OR...

PHOSPHORESCENT PAINT! SPECIAL FOR GHOSTS!

AND THIS IS A UV LIGHT PROJECTOR TO TRIGGER ITS LUMINESCENCE...

CHEMISTRY AND PHYSICS. NOTHING MAGICAL HERE. LET'S SEE BEHIND THIS DOOR...

30A

HAAAAAA! LADY MARY!

A DUMMY! GOOD GRIEF, WHAT A FRIGHT! STILL, THIS IS THE DRESS LADY MARY'S GHOST WAS WEARING...

THE PLOT THICKENS YET AGAIN. I...

CLICK

?

NO! DON'T SHOOT!

30B

STOP TREMBLING... WHATEVER THE OTHERS MAY SAY, I'VE NEVER KILLED ANYONE!

I DON'T DOUBT IT, BUT WHY THE DUMMY? AND WHERE DID YOU GET THIS DRESS?

YOU SHOULD SAY THIS SHROUD; BECAUSE IT WAS IN HER WEDDING DRESS THAT THEY BURIED LADY MARY.

SURELY YOU DIDN'T GO AND STRIP HER OF...

NO! ONE MORNING I FOUND IT OUTSIDE MY DOOR! IT WAS MARY WHO CAME AND ENTRUSTED ME WITH THIS LAST ANCHOR TO HER EARTHLY LIFE...

THEY WEREN'T EXAGGE-RATING... HE IS MAD!

A LITTLE LATER...

TWO BLACK QUEENS... COINCIDENCE!

FATE HAS NO USE FOR COINCIDENCES.

THERE WILL SOON BE **TWO DEAD WOMEN** AT LOCH CASTLE!

TWO?

51A

THE CARDS ALREADY SENTENCED ONE TWENTY YEARS AGO. AS FOR THE OTHER, MARY WILL LEAD HER WHERE SHE'LL STOP MEDDLING...

"TWO ROSES ON A BRANCH"... THAT MESSAGE WAS FROM YOU?

I WANTED TO PUT YOU ON THE RIGHT TRACK... DO YOU LIKE RABBIT STEW?

YES!

ACCORDING TO THE CARDS, IT'S THE ARRIVAL OF A FOURTH QUEEN THAT WILL MAKE EVERY-THING CLEAR AT LOCH CASTLE.

THERE ARE ALWAYS FOUR QUEENS IN A DECK...

BUT THERE IS ONLY ONE MURDERER IN LOCH CASTLE, AND BY COMBINING OUR HANDS WE'LL FIND HIM.

SHOW ME YOURS...

AN HOUR LATER, YOKO IS BACK AT THE CASTLE.

IT WASN'T EASY TO CONVINCE THAT CRACKPOT MAC NAB!

51B

33

AH! THE SPARE TYRE HAS ARRIVED.

HONK!

VIC! AT LAST!

SAY, YOU LOOK RATHER HAPPY THERE... WHAT HAPPENED TO YOUR PROBLEM?

I'M JUST GLAD TO SEE YOU...

... BUT THAT DOESN'T CHANGE THE DEPTH OF THE MYSTERY... LET'S LEAVE HERE SOONEST; I'LL EXPLAIN ON THE WAY.

AH! WE'LL FINALLY BE RID OF THIS LITTLE MEDDLER!

32A

HALF AN HOUR LATER...

SIR WILLIAM SENDS HIS APOLOGIES; HE HAD TO LEAVE...

WE'LL BE COMING BACK THIS WAY IN THREE DAYS, AND WE'LL STOP TO GIVE OUR THANKS TO SIR WILLIAM...

OH? VERY WELL.

FAREWELL, YOKO. DO NOT COME BACK HERE... IT'S BETTER FOR ME.

BETTER FOR YOU? THAT, CECILIA, IS FAR FROM CERTAIN...

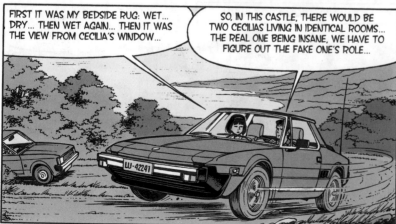

FIRST IT WAS MY BEDSIDE RUG: WET... DRY... THEN WET AGAIN... THEN IT WAS THE VIEW FROM CECILIA'S WINDOW...

SO, IN THIS CASTLE, THERE WOULD BE TWO CECILIAS LIVING IN IDENTICAL ROOMS... THE REAL ONE BEING INSANE, WE HAVE TO FIGURE OUT THE FAKE ONE'S ROLE...

IT'S EITHER TO ENCOURAGE BELIEF IN THE REAL CECILIA'S MADNESS, OR TO PROTECT HER BY DIRECTING MAC NAB'S VENGEANCE ONTO THE FAKE ... IT WOULD BE LOGICAL IF I DIDN'T HAVE THE CONVICTION THAT SHE WAS USED TO PREPARE AN ODIOUS CRIME! WE'RE HEADING FOR THE COAST. I NEED SOME FISHING SUPPLIES...

YOU DO? WHAT FOR?

32B

AND WHEN, ONCE MORE, THE NIGHT IS HIDING EVERYTHING AROUND LOCH CASTLE...

IN THE RUINS OF THE ABBEY...

WILL IT HOLD?

A JAPANESE ELEPHANT COULD HANG FROM IT!

NOW WE NEED TO BRING THE REST OF THE EQUIPMENT BEFORE FULL NIGHT, AND IT'S A LONG WALK TO WHERE WE HID THE CAR.

IT'S TIME I GO AND CONVINCE CECILIA N°2...

WHAT IF SHE'S IN LEAGUE WITH THE OTHERS?

I DON'T THINK SO, VIC. CECILIA'S DOUBLE HAS A SECRET I'D LIKE TO DISCOVER.

AND, LEAVING VIC AND POL, YOKO MAKES HER WAY TO THE CASTLE THROUGH THE TUNNEL.

FIVE MINUTES LATER.

AH! I'M FINALLY UNDER THE RIVER.

TO THE LEFT, THE ARMS ROOM... STRAIGHT AHEAD, "CECILIA'S" ROOM.

PULL OUT, THEN SLIDE... THERE!

GOOD EVENING, MISS!

YOKO!

YOU PROMISED YOU WOULDN'T COME BACK!

I MAY HAVE PROMISED CECILIA.... BUT NOT YOU! WHAT'S YOUR NAME AGAIN, PLEASE?

I COULD FEEL IT—YOU GUESSED EVERYTHING! OH, IF ONLY YOU KNEW...

I'D KNOW A LOT MORE IF YOU TALKED. WHAT'S YOUR REAL NAME?

MY NAME IS MARGARET. THERE WERE, IN THE COMPANY I WORKED FOR, SEVERAL ILLEGAL MONEY TRANSFERS UNDER MY SIGNATURE. I COULDN'T PROVE MY INNOCENCE...

MY EMPLOYER, SIR WILLIAM, OFFERED TO FORGET IT ALL IN EXCHANGE FOR A PECULIAR JOB: BECOME A DOUBLE FOR HIS DAUGHTER CECILIA, WHO HAD LOST HER MIND, AND TOWARDS WHOM I HAD AN UNCANNY RESEMBLANCE.

34A

I ACCEPTED, AND LITTLE BY LITTLE DISCOVERED THAT I WAS IN FACT BEING USED AS BAIT FOR THIS NUTTER MAC NAB, BECAUSE SIR WILLIAM WANTED REVENGE ON HIM...

AND THE GHOST?

A HOAX, TO PANIC MAC NAB... AND I HELPED CREATE IT.

THE "LADY IN BLACK": WAS THAT YOU AS WELL?

YES, I WAS HOPING TO LEAD YOU TO CECILIA WITHOUT BREAKING MY WORD. I'M SCARED... I'M MISSING SOMETHING!

OH? WELL, WHY DON'T YOU TAKE ME TO THE REAL CECILIA!

A SHORT WHILE LATER...

THE MOTOR IS CONTROLLED FROM HERE.

THERE! THE PANEL SLIDES, UNCOVERING THE RIGHT DOOR WHILE HIDING THE LEFT ONE.

BROOM

GOOD EVENING, MISS TSUNO. BACK SO SOON?

34B

I DON'T SEE YOUR CHARMING COMPANIONS. COULD YOU HAVE LEFT THEM IN THE DARK?

I'M NOT IN THE HABIT OF EXPOSING A THEORY BEFORE I VERIFY IT.

AND ONCE THIS CERTAINTY IS ACQUIRED, WHAT DO YOU INTEND TO DO?

WARN CECILIA THAT SOMEONE ELSE IS IN MORTAL DANGER IN HER PLACE. IT'S REVOLTING!

I'M AFRAID THE PROGRAM HAS JUST CHANGED QUITE A LOT FOR YOU, MISS TSUNO.

OH!

WHAT IS THIS? I DON'T UNDERSTAND!

YOU WILL SOON, MARGARET. UP! TOWARDS THE RIGHT WING, THE CORNER TOWER.

AS FOR YOU, MISS TSUNO, YOU WILL BE DELIGHTED TO MEET A GHOST AGAIN.

I WARNED YOU. YOU'RE GOING TO PAY DEARLY FOR YOUR CURIOSITY!

LIKE YOU MUST HAVE PAID DEARLY FOR ALL THIS...

"ALL THIS" IS MADE IN MY COMPANY'S ELECTRONICS DEPARTMENT. AND IT'S ALL ABOUT THREE-DIMENSIONAL CINEMA.

AND IT'S MARGARET, DRESSED AS LADY MARY, WHO HELPED SHOOT THAT MOVIE.

I HAD NO IDEA WHAT THEY WOULD DO WITH IT!

I WOULD SAY: THE HOLOGRAPHIC BAND. FOUR TRACKS FEEDING AS MANY CAMERAS TO PRODUCE THE 3D PICTURE YOU CHASED LAST NIGHT.

ALL THIS FOR MAC NAB...

WRONG! IT'S CECILIA THEY'RE DRIVING INSANE!

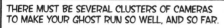

THERE MUST BE SEVERAL CLUSTERS OF CAMERAS TO MAKE YOUR GHOST RUN SO WELL, AND SO FAR.

WITH THESE MINIATURISED CAMERAS, THE LENS IS THE BULKIEST PART.

HOW DOES SUCH A SMALL PROJECTOR PRODUCE ENOUGH LUMINOSITY?

THE IMAGE IS SENT TO IT BY FIBRE OPTIC CABLE. EVEN OVER A KILOMETRE AWAY THERE'S NO LOSS OF LUMINESCENCE.

YOUR "GHOST" ALWAYS KEEPS THE SAME DISTANCE AWAY FROM ITS PURSUERS?

THE WHOLE COURSE IS SWEPT BY A LASER RANGEFINDER, AND THE GHOST SPEEDS UP OR DOWN WHENEVER ITS PURSUER DOES.

ALL THE DATA IS TRANSFERRED TO THE COMPUTER THAT CONTROLS THE OPERATION. ENOUGH THEORY: PLEASE PUT YOUR HANDS BEHIND YOUR BACK.

DON'T DO IT!

YOU TREAT HER LIKE A CRIMINAL!

EASY, MARGARET. YOUR TURN IS COMING.

THESE OPTICAL FIBRES MAKE EXCELLENT BONDS...

SHE'S EITHER SINCERE OR A GREAT ACTRESS.

SHORTLY AFTERWARDS... THERE. AS A SPECIAL FAVOUR, YOU'LL BE SEATED FOR THE SHOW.

ONE LAST DETAIL...

I AM FORCED TO SILENCE YOUR PRETTY VOICE.

MMMM

IT'S THE ROLE OF YOUR LIFE... ACTRESS AND SPECTATOR AT THE SAME TIME!

THE ACTRESS WILL DO HER BEST, POOR FOOL, TO HELP YOU FALL INTO YOUR OWN TRAP... AH, THE LIGHTS ARE DIMMING. LADY MARY WILL SOON APPEAR.

BUT FIRST, LET'S CHECK IF THE STAR IS ON STAGE.

I'LL START THE PICTURE IN FIVE MINUTES, BUT I'LL GIVE YOU THIRTY.

THAT'LL DO.

SHE IS!

FROM NOW ON, ANY MISTAKE I MAKE COULD BE FATAL...

CECILIA HAS SEEN HER. SOON HER DOOR WILL OPEN AND, LIKE YESTERDAY, SHE WILL FOLLOW HER MOTHER'S SHADE.

AND YOU WILL NO LONGER BE ABLE TO STOP HER. COME ON, TO THE ABBEY. WE MUST BE ON TIME FOR THE FINALE...

ANGLE RIGHT, BY THE RIVER, TO AVOID ALERTING THE DOGS.

AND SOON THE DOCTOR AND HIS PRISONER ARE AT THE CHAPEL...

THERE, IN THAT CORNER.

AND YOU, BE QUIET. ONE WORD, ONE MOVE, AND I BLOW YOUR BRAINS OUT.

MMMM

SEVERAL LONG MINUTES CRAWL BY... THEN, SUDDENLY...

HERE SHE COMES!

DON'T MOVE!

OUT OF BREATH, CECILIA RUNS INTO THE CHAPEL.

LIKE YOKO THE NIGHT BEFORE, SHE HESITATES IN SURPRISE, THEN BOLTS TOWARDS THE GHOST AND ITS OUTSTRETCHED HANDS.

AND SUDDENLY THE GROUND DISAPPEARS FROM UNDER CECILIA'S FEET.

QUIET!

MMMM

AAAAAAAA!

WORRIED, YOKO PEERS INTO THE NIGHT'S SILENCE.

I CAN'T HEAR ANYTHING! PLEASE LET HER BE...

CHLOROFORM! DON'T BREATHE IN! DON'T...

AND, LIFTING YOKO IN HIS ARMS, THE SINISTER DOCTOR CARRIES HER TOWARDS THE CHASM WHERE CECILIA HAS VANISHED.

THAT'LL DO.

LET'S REMOVE BONDS AND GAG.

40

THE DOGS! JOHN WILL RELEASE THEM SOON.

WOOF!

WOOF!

YOKO! OH, WELL DONE!

SHHH!

GOODBYE, MISS TSUNO!

WOOF

IN THE MEANTIME, YOUR "FAKE CECILIA" FAINTED...

SHE'S NOT THE FAKE; SHE'S THE REAL ONE!

SHE IS?

QUICKLY—WE DON'T HAVE MUCH TIME LEFT FOR OUR SET-UP... POL, BRING THE NET IN.

THAT'S WHAT I WAS BUSY DOING!

YOU ALMOST WORKED WITHOUT A NET... I'M STILL SHAKING ABOUT IT...

TO BE QUITE HONEST, SO AM I... BEFORE, DURING AND AFTER!

A FEW MINUTES LATER...

THIS WAY, SIR WILLIAM!

WOOF!

WOOF!

DOWN THERE, SIR, I CAN SEE A SHAPE ON THE GROUND...

MMMM

GO AND... GO AND CHECK, JOHN... I CANNOT.

41

AS JOHN PROCEEDS DOWN TO THE CRYPT...

I KNEW THIS WOULD ALL END HORRIBLY!

IT'S REALLY HER... OH, SUCH A CURSE UPON US ALL!

MISS CECILIA! THIS IS SO HORRIBLE. I...

... SIR WILLIAM, LEFT ALONE, LETS HIS EXPRESSION TURN TRIUMPHANT.

POOR JOHN IS IN FOR QUITE A SURPRISE!

GOODNESS GRACIOUS!

40A

JOHN! IS SHE...?

DEAD? NO, SIR! FOR THIS ONE WAS NEVER ALIVE!

ANOTHER ONE OF MAC NAB'S FOUL JOKES!

A DUMMY! THAT'S IMPOSSIBLE!

WHAT WERE YOU HOPING TO FIND DOWN THERE, SIR WILLIAM?

40B

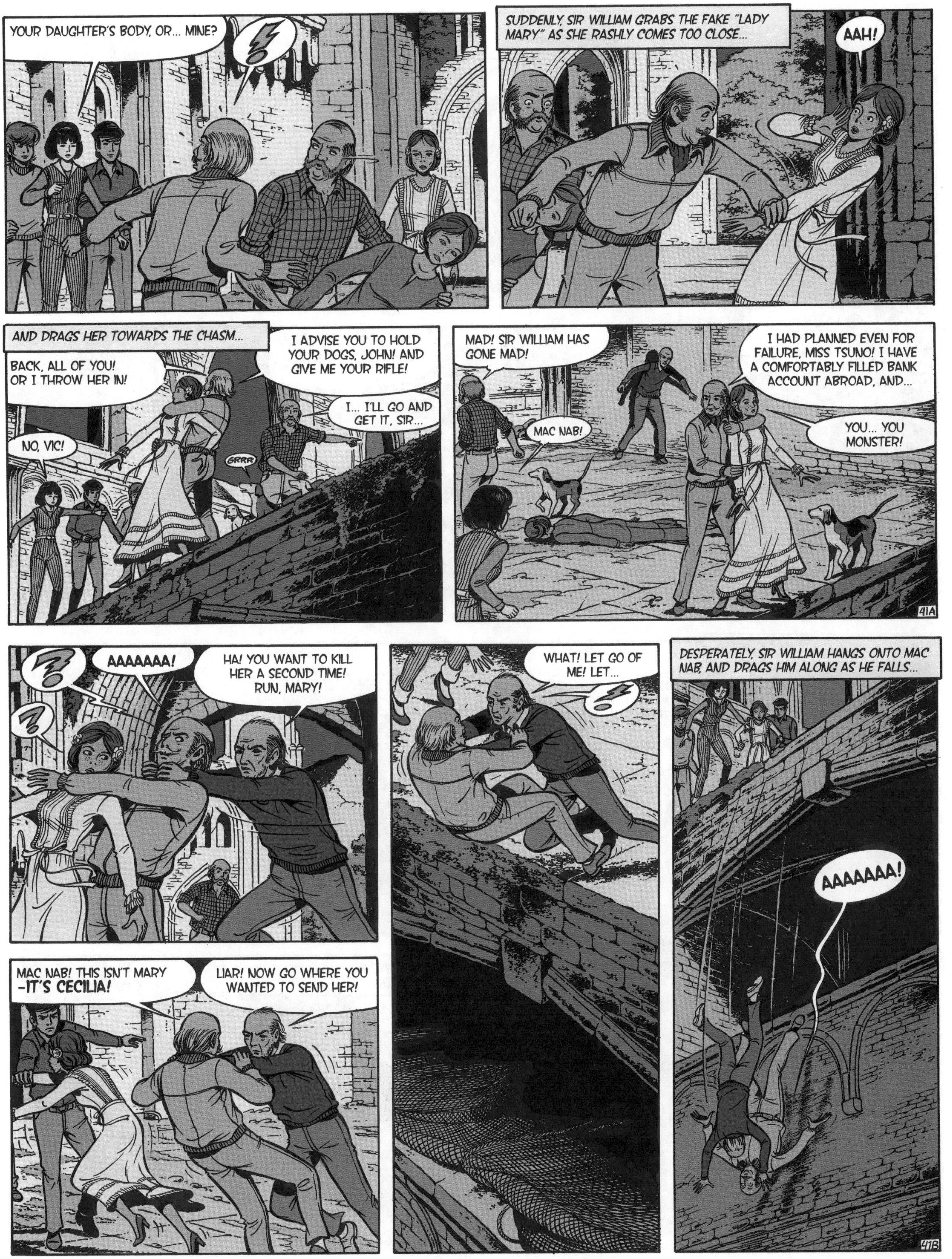
YOUR DAUGHTER'S BODY, OR... MINE?
SUDDENLY, SIR WILLIAM GRABS THE FAKE "LADY MARY" AS SHE RASHLY COMES TOO CLOSE...
AAH!
AND DRAGS HER TOWARDS THE CHASM...
BACK, ALL OF YOU! OR I THROW HER IN!
I ADVISE YOU TO HOLD YOUR DOGS, JOHN! AND GIVE ME YOUR RIFLE!
I... I'LL GO AND GET IT, SIR...
NO, VIC!
GRRR
MAD! SIR WILLIAM HAS GONE MAD!
I HAD PLANNED EVEN FOR FAILURE, MISS TSUNO! I HAVE A COMFORTABLY FILLED BANK ACCOUNT ABROAD, AND...
MAC NAB!
YOU... YOU MONSTER!
41A
AAAAAAA!
HA! YOU WANT TO KILL HER A SECOND TIME! RUN, MARY!
MAC NAB! THIS ISN'T MARY -IT'S CECILIA!
LIAR! NOW GO WHERE YOU WANTED TO SEND HER!
WHAT! LET GO OF ME! LET...
DESPERATELY, SIR WILLIAM HANGS ONTO MAC NAB, AND DRAGS HIM ALONG AS HE FALLS...
AAAAAAA!
41B

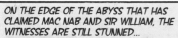

ON THE EDGE OF THE ABYSS THAT HAS CLAIMED MAC NAB AND SIR WILLIAM, THE WITNESSES ARE STILL STUNNED...

I CAN'T HEAR A THING.

IT WOULD BE A MIRACLE IF YOU DID!

OH, IT'S HORRIBLE!

BE STRONG, CECILIA.

POL, HEAD DOWN AND SEE IF ANYTHING CAN STILL BE DONE FOR THEM.

WHOA, GRIM DUTY, THAT!

DEPENDING ON WHAT POL FINDS, JOHN, YOU WILL CALL AN AMBULANCE, OR ONLY THE POLICE. I'LL LEAVE CECILIA IN YOUR HANDS. VIC AND I WILL DEAL WITH THAT VILLAIN OF A DOCTOR.

R... RIGHT YOU ARE, MISS!

THE FIRST ROSE IS SAFE... THAT STILL LEAVES THE SECOND ONE, AND I'M WORRIED ABOUT HER.

BACK AT THE CASTLE, EVENTS ARE SPEEDING UP...

YES, MY DEAR MARGARET, BY ELIMINATING CECILIA, SIR WILLIAM GETS HOLD OF HER FORTUNE. IT BECOMES A PERFECT CRIME WHEN THE LAST WITNESS DISAPPEARS! THEREFORE, MY FINAL TASK IS TO DISPOSE OF YOU. HOWEVER, THERE IS A BETTER OPTION...

YOU REMAIN ALIVE IN A SAFE PLACE, AND THE TWO OF US BLACKMAIL SIR WILLIAM. CHOOSE, THEN: FORTUNE AND LIFE, OR... DEATH!

I'D RATHER DIE THAN SERVE A MURDERER!

DON'T WORRY, MARGARET. THIS DEVIL WON'T KILL ANYONE ELSE!

YOKO!

SUDDENLY THE DOCTOR WHIRLS ROUND AND...

LOOK OUT!

SHTOCK

POK

ONE DROP OF THIS COMPOUND KILLS, HE SAID... YOU WERE LUCKY!

SO WERE YOU!

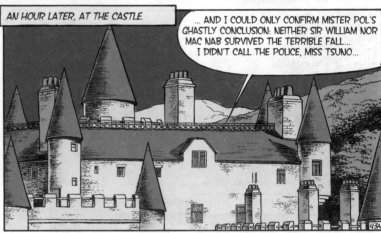

AN HOUR LATER, AT THE CASTLE.

... AND I COULD ONLY CONFIRM MISTER POL'S GHASTLY CONCLUSION: NEITHER SIR WILLIAM NOR MAC NAB SURVIVED THE TERRIBLE FALL... I DIDN'T CALL THE POLICE, MISS TSUNO...

... BECAUSE I BELIEVE MISS CECILIA SHOULD BE THE FIRST TO HEAR YOUR EXPLANATIONS...

IT'S GOING TO HURT, CECILIA, BUT IT'S BETTER TO GET IT OVER WITH.

GO AHEAD!

WHEN, TWENTY YEARS AGO, MAC NAB SEES LADY MARY, THE WOMAN HE LOVES, MARRY SIR BRIAN, HE PREDICTS THAT THE COUPLE WILL MEET A TRAGIC END. HE EVEN GOES SO FAR AS TO ADD THAT THEIR CHILD TO COME WILL NOT REACH ADULTHOOD!

NO ONE TOOK HIM SERIOUSLY.

NO. NOT UNTIL YOUR FATHER IS KILLED IN A CAR CRASH. ALL SEE IN THIS ACCIDENT MAC NAB'S VENGEANCE. IT DRIVES YOUR MOTHER INSANE, AND SIR WILLIAM EASILY MARRIES HER, THUS MANAGING HER WEALTH. YOU WERE FIVE.

SO LONG AGO...

WITH LADY MARY GONE MAD, HE ELIMINATES HER. A DRUGGED HORSE, A ROPE, A FALL... AND ANOTHER CRIME PINNED ON MAC NAB, WHO IS SET FREE FOR LACK OF EVIDENCE. THERE ARE NO MORE OBSTACLES; YOU ARE YOUNG, AND SIR WILLIAM PLAYS THE EXEMPLARY FATHER TO YOU. ALAS, THE YEARS FLY BY QUICKLY...

YOU WILL SOON COME OF AGE, AND INTO FULL CONTROL OF YOUR INHERITANCE. SIR WILLIAM FEARS THAT... HE ENLISTS A CORRUPT DOCTOR WHO, USING DRUGS, SLOWLY UNBALANCES YOUR MIND.

TO HIS AMAZEMENT, SIR WILLIAM DISCOVERS AMONG HIS EMPLOYEES YOUR EXACT DOUBLE, MARGARET. USING TRUMPED-UP MISAPPROPRIATION CHARGES, HE FORCES HER TO PARTICIPATE IN HIS FIENDISH PLAN... SHE WILL HELP CREATE **THE GHOST** WHOSE **PREY** YOU WILL BE!

I WAS SUPPOSED TO TAKE CECILIA'S PLACE WHEN HER MADNESS MADE HER UNSUITED FOR SOCIAL OCCASIONS. LATER, WHEN I HAD TO DRESS UP AS LADY MARY TO RECORD THE HOLOGRAPHIC IMAGES, I FEARED   I WOULD ATTRACT MAC NAB'S HATRED...

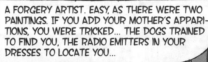

AND IF, DURING THAT DINNER, I WAS SO HORRIBLE TO YOU, IT WAS TO ALLAY SUSPICIONS AND BETTER NUDGE YOU TOWARDS THE REAL CECILIA. I HOPED THAT, ONCE THE TRUTH WAS DISCOVERED, THIS GAME WOULD STOP.

IN THIS GAME, YOU WERE, FROM THE VERY START, SENTENCED TO DEATH.

THIS IS INSANE! YOU RISKED YOUR LIFE... AND MINE, FOR A LITTLE MONEY!

LIKE YOU, CECILIA, I LOST MY MOTHER WHEN STILL VERY YOUNG. BUT MY ORPHANAGE WASN'T A CASTLE. THAT MONEY WAS MY TICKET TO A NEW LIFE...

MY COUSINS FROM AUSTRALIA OFFERED FOR ME TO COME LIVE WITH THEM. THEY RAISE SHEEP... PAYING FOR THE TRIP IS THE PROBLEM.

PAH. SOMEONE AROUND HERE OWES YOU THAT MUCH.

BUT... WHAT ABOUT THE PAINTING TOUCHED UP DURING THE NIGHT...?

A FORGERY ARTIST. EASY, AS THERE WERE TWO PAINTINGS. IF YOU ADD YOUR MOTHER'S APPARITIONS, YOU WERE TRICKED... THE DOGS TRAINED TO FIND YOU, THE RADIO EMITTERS IN YOUR DRESSES TO LOCATE YOU...

... MAC NAB BRAINWASHED INTO BEING THIS NEW CRIME'S PERFECT SUSPECT... BELIEVE ME, CECILIA: WITHOUT MARGARET, YOU'D BE DEAD BY NOW!

I AM SORRY, MARGARET. AND IF YOU THINK YOU CAN FIND HAPPINESS IN AUSTRALIA, I'LL PAY FOR YOUR TICKET.

THANK YOU.

A MONTH AFTER THESE EVENTS...

THIS CAN'T GO ON, VIC. CECILIA INTENDS TO PROVE HER GRATITUDE BY GIVING ME A DRESS EVERY DAY!

SHE'S GOT GOOD TASTE, AND THEY SUIT YOU!

THANK YOU FOR SAYING SO, BUT SOCIETY LIFE ISN'T MY STYLE... ALL IN ALL, I'D RATHER BE IN AUSTRALIA WITH MARGARET, COUNTING SHEEP...

THAT'D PUT YOU TO SLEEP. NO! I HAVE SOMETHING BETTER FOR YOU. A TICKET TO HONG KONG, FOR EXAMPLE...

DO YOU MEAN MY FATHER CALLED AND YOU SAID NOTHING?

I WAS WAITING FOR CONFIRMATION. SOON WE'LL BE BACK TO ASIA, FOR MORE OF THOSE ADVENTURES YOU HAVE SUCH A KNACK FOR!

THE END

TEXT AND DRAWING
R Leloup
COLOURING: BEATRICE
-Studio LEONARDO

ON THE EDGE OF LIFE

1 - ON THE EDGE OF LIFE

THE TIME SPIRAL

2 - THE TIME SPIRAL

JULY 2009

THE PREY AND THE GHOST

3 - THE PREY AND THE GHOST

DAUGHTER OF THE WIND

4 - DAUGHTER OF THE WIND

9th CINEBOOK
The 9th Art Publisher

www.cinebook.com

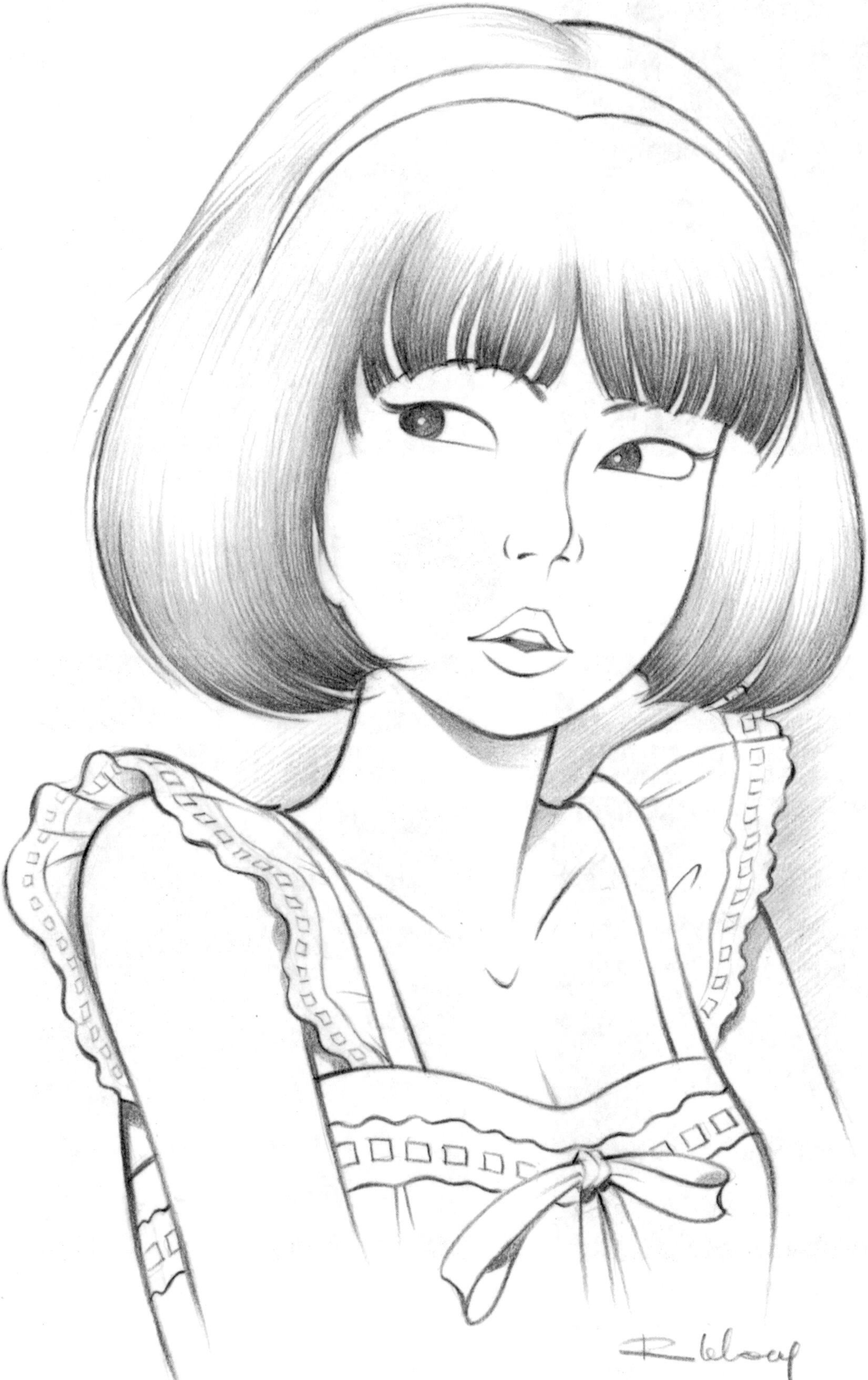